American *Cat*-alogue

1.
MARY HUNTER
August Edouart
dated April 30, 1841
Washington
Silhouette   8½″ x 4½
Collection of Jack Anspa

American *Cat*-alogue

The Cat in American Folk Art

Bruce Johnson

A Flare Book/Published by Avon Books
In Association with
Museum of American Folk Art

AVON BOOKS
A division of
The Hearst Corporation
959 Eighth Avenue
New York, New York 10019

Library of Congress Catalogue Card Number: 75–39821
ISBN: 0-380-00590-5

First Flare Printing, January, 1976
Third Printing

FLARE TRADEMARK REG. U.S. PAT. OFF. AND IN
OTHER COUNTRIES, MARCA REGISTRADA, HECHO EN
U.S.A.

Photography for the Museum of American
Folk Art by Noel Allum

Book designed by Ellen Blissman

Printed in the U. S. A.

This catalogue is dedicated to my good friends:
Blue,
Sam,
Larry,
Jerry,
Joe,
Pendelton,
Maurice (the Gray Catsby),
Dippy,
Whitey,
Midnight,
Joe Willie,
Maum,
Purrless.

2. SMUTT
Artist unknown
mid 19th century
found in Fryeburg, Maine
oil on canvas   18″ x 21½″
Private Collection

3. CAT WITH MOUSE
Artist unknown
19th century
oil on paper mounted on wood with wax
22¼″ x 28″
Collection of the Robert Hull Fleming
Museum, bequest of Henry Schnackenberg

Artists often convey a message or create a mood with iconography. Many animals because of repeated reference in mythology, literature, and art have come to have iconographical meanings. For instance, the owl was used in Renaissance paintings and prints to convey a sense of evil: the presence of an owl in a Dürer print always indicates foreboding. These animals acquire such meanings from their character, particularly those traits which seem to be human.

The Museum has assembled examples of American folk art which depict the cat in many and varied forms. It is important to note where the cat is used and not used, and examine why it has been used so often, looking at its iconographical and artistic use.

Perhaps it is because of their penetrating, alert stare, perhaps it is because of the elegance, sureness, gracefulness, and pride with which a cat strolls through a parlor or moves through an alley, or perhaps it is because they are wild and domestic at the same time; whatever the reason, the cat has been respected as a creature of mystery since the time of the Egyptians, and has appeared in the art of almost every culture —sometimes as deity, sometimes as devil.

American folk artists have used every kind of cat in every kind of pose in every kind of artform—black cats (fig. 38), white cats (fig. 11), tabbies (fig. 14), short hairs (fig. 72), long hairs (fig. 108), sleeping cats (fig. 55), sitting cats (fig. 15), playing kittens (fig. 44), mouse hunters (fig. 68), lap cats (fig. 20), hissing cats (fig. 78)—on canvas (fig. 90), on whaleteeth (fig. 8), on fireboards (fig. 111), on quilts (fig. 39), on hooked rugs (fig. 112), as pottery (fig. 13), and even as a carrousel figure (fig. 107).

In many paintings, the cat is the sole subject. In others, he is painted as the companion of an adult or child (fig. 42). Some cats are difficult to find because they are hiding (fig. 97), or in the background (fig. 61), but always they are important to the composition and action of the work.

Although the cat is so ubiquitous in child portraiture that he is often not noticed, his presence is necessary to the success of the painting. No matter how tiny and seemingly insignificant, if the cat is taken away, the composition loses its vitality and the painting becomes stagnant and less interesting. Cover up the cats in fig. 40 and fig. 93, and it becomes clear that the cat adds depth to a rather flat painting.

Though the cats in these paintings are painted very realistically and probably were the inseparable companions of the children, early limners recognized the artistic value of using a cat. It is interesting to note how often the artist captures the individual nature of the cat better than that of the child (fig. 53).

In some pieces, such as the quilt (fig. 22) and the wall shelf (fig. 87), the cat is reduced to a stylized organic shape that is easy to make and easy to recognize. This is a useful convention for the folk artist because it gives vitality to an otherwise less interesting geometric or floral pattern. Here again, the cat form is used as an artistic device with no obvious symbolic significance.

Figures 32 and 81 are stereotype halloween-black cats and are associated with the witch-cat myths in American folklore. Witches are believed to be able to transform themselves into cats. Cats are also famous as companions or "familiars" of witches and sorcerers. Most sculptures of this type do not appear until the twentieth century because earlier artists were superstitious and feared that the cat's image would summon evil spirits.

On the other hand, the cat is often a symbol of the home. One popular convention shows a cat in front of the hearth, as in the tray (fig. 50), and the fireboard (fig. 111), and in many hooked rugs. Another shows them as our friends, the mouse catchers.

But, the cat is missing from many forms of folk art, probably for reasons of superstition.

Maritime art has surprisingly few cats in a culture so full of cat terminology and superstition (catboats, catfall, cathead, cat-o'-nine-tails, cat rig, cat's-paw, and catwalk are all nautical terms). Sailors often watched cats because their preening habits were believed to foretell the weather. But, cats are rarely used by sailors in their artwork. Either sailors were more interested in mermaids and anchors, or cats were taboo as artistic subject matter.

Notwithstanding the Lewis Miller pediment (fig. 58), on which there is a very eerie cat, cats are rarely found in Pennsylvania German art, such as frakturs and pottery. Perhaps the very superstitious Pennsylvania Germans, steeped in beliefs of "hexerei," also feared using the cat. Edward Hicks

4.
CAT WEATHERVANE
Artist unknown
c. 1930
iron   17¼″ x 27½″
Collection of Joe and Ellen Wetherell

only used the cat once in all his animal paintings: in the background of David Twining's farm, a cat with an arched back fights a dog.

Although there are many superstitions relating cats to weather and although animals of all kinds appear as weathervanes, cat weathervanes are almost unheard of. The two examples depicted here (fig. 4) and (fig. 70) are late, and one was a carrousel figure later converted to a weathervane by an unsuperstitious catlover. Does this mean that a cat on top of a house causes bad luck? Why can a cat be on a rug inside a house but not be a weathervane outside? Perhaps the reasons derive from superstition, or it may be that the cat's symbolic connection to the hearth makes it unsuitable for vanes which usually depict outside animals such as cows, roosters, horses, and pigs.

Cats are popular subjects of the folktales and superstitions of America. Many of these stories have their origin in Europe or Africa, but over the years have become very American. Often the same story appears in many different places, each regional storyteller adding his own touch.

Few other animals are so prominent in our folk culture, and we can assume that the cat will always be an inspiration to American folk artists.

5. CAT THEOREM
    Artist unknown
    early 19th century
    paint on velvet   8¾″ x 10¾″
    Collection of Jack and Gretchen Sl

CAT—578

*To dream that a vicious cat attacks you and you are
unable to drive it away, foretells that you have desperate
enemies who will make it a point to blacken your
reputation and cause the loss of property through fire,
from which legal difficulties may arise. If you are able
to scare the cat away, you will overcome great obstacles.
To dream of a cat that appears tame and gentle, speaks
of deceptive friends who may not injure you or harm
you, but annoy you in matters pertaining to gossiping.*

—Prince Ali Lucky Five Star Fortune Telling Dream Book.

6. FIGURE OF A CAT
Attributed to Samuel Bell
mid 19th century
Strasburg, Virginia
redware   6¼"
Collection of Mr. and Mrs. Boyd Headley, Jr.

CARNIVAL CAT
Artist unknown
early 20th century
papier mâché with velvet cloth tail   21″
Collection of James Mincemoyer

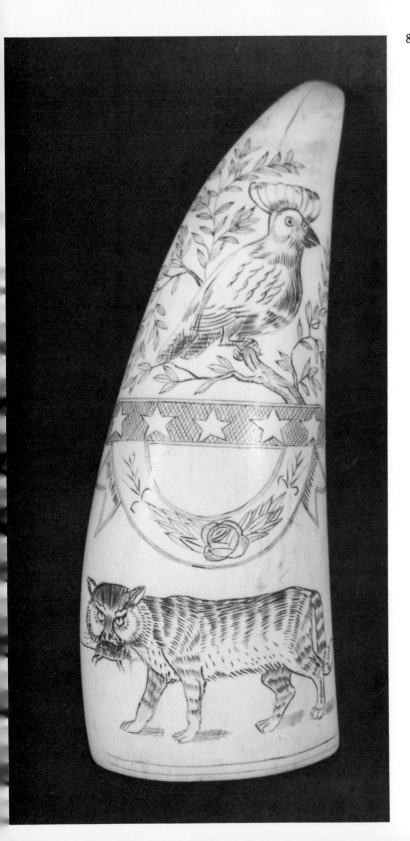

8. SCRIMSHAW
    cat with mouse
    Artist unknown
    c. 1910
    engraved whale's tooth   6
    Collection of the Ships of the S
    Museum, Savannah, Georgia

    Part of a pair.

A three color cat prevents fires.

9. CAT AND KITTENS
    Artist unknown
    c. 1872/c. 1883
    millboard   12″ x 13⅞″
    National Gallery of Art. Gift of
    Edgar William and Bernice Chrysler Garbisch

CAT PORTRAIT
Attributed to Miss Elizabeth Forbes
late 19th century
Pennsylvania
pastel on paper   13″ x 17¾″
Collection of Dr. and Mrs. Alexander Shevlin

11.   WHITE CAT
      Artist unknown
      1900
      oil on board   12″ x 10″
      Collection of Steve Miller

12. CAT ON A WINDOW SILL
    Artist unknown
    late 19th century
    found in Ohio
    oil on wood panel   10″ x 12¾″
    Collection of Harry and Betty Waldman

WAIT TILL EMMETT COMES

Once upon a time there was an old colored preacher who was riding to a church he served at some distance from his home when night overtook him and he got lost. As it grew darker and darker, he began to be afraid, but he bolstered up his courage by saying every little while, "De Lawd will sholy take care ob me." By and by he saw a light, and riding up to it, he discovered that it came from the cabin of another colored man. Getting off his horse and tying it to a fence stake, he knocked at the cabin door. When the owner opened it, the old preacher told his trouble and asked to stay all night. The colored man replied, "Well, Pahson, I suttinly would like ter keep yo' all night, but my cabin hain't got but one room in it an' I got a wife an' ten chilluns. Dey jis' ain't no place fo' yo' ter stay."

The old preacher leaned up against the side of the house and in a woebegone voice said, "Well, I guess de Lawd will sholy take care ob me." Then slowly untying his horse and getting on him, he started to ride on. But the owner of the cabin stopped him and said, "Pahson, yo' might sleep in de big house. Da' ain't nobody up da' an' de doo' ain't locked. Yo' can put yo' hoss in de ba'n an' give him some hay an' den you can walk right in. You'll fin' a big fiahplace in de big room an' de wood all laid fo' de fiah. Yo' can jis' tech a match to it an' make yo'self cumfable." As the old preacher began to disappear into the dark, the other called out, "But, Pahson, I didn' tell you dat de house is haunted." The old man hesitated for a moment, but finally rode away, saying, "Well, I guess de Lawd sholy will take care ob me."

When he arrived at the place, he put his horse in the barn and gave him some hay. Then he moved over to the house, and sure enough, he found it unlocked. In the big room he found a great fireplace with an immense amount of wood all laid ready to kindle. He touched a match to it and in a few minutes had a big roaring fire. He lighted an oil lamp that was on a table and drawing up a big easy chair, he sat down and began to read his Bible. By and by the fire burnt down, leaving a great heap of red-hot coals.

The old man continued to read his Bible until he was aroused by a sudden noise in one corner of the room. Looking up, he saw a big cat, and it was a black cat, too. Slowly stretching himself, the cat walked over to the fire and flung himself into the bed of red-hot coals. Tossing them up with his feet, he rolled over in them, then

Coffin, Tristram P. and Cohen, Hennig. FOLKLORE IN AMERICA. Garden City, New York: Doubleday and Company, 1966, pages 26-28.

shaking the ashes off himself, he walked over to the old man and sat down to one side of him, near his feet, looked up at him with his fiery-green eyes, licked out his long, red tongue, lashed his tail, and said, "Wait till Emmett comes."

The old man kept on reading his Bible, when all at once he heard a noise in another corner of the room, and looking up he saw another black cat, big as a dog. Slowly stretching himself, he walked over to the bed of coals, threw himself into them, tumbled all around, and tossed them with his feet. Then he got up, shook the ashes off himself, walked over to the old man, and sat down near his feet on the opposite side from the first cat. He looked up at him with his fiery-green eyes, licked out his long, red tongue, lashed his tail, and asked the first cat, "Now what shall we do wid him?" The first cat answered, "Wait till Emmett comes."

The old man kept on reading his Bible and, in a little while, he heard a noise in a third corner of the room, and looking up, he saw a cat black as night and as big as a calf. He, too, got up, stretched himself, walked over to the bed of coals, and threw himself into them. He rolled over and over in them, tossed them with his feet, took some into his mouth, chewed them up and spat them out again. Then, shaking the ashes off himself, he walked over to the old colored man and sat down right in front of him. He looked up at him with his fiery-green eyes, licked out his long, red tongue, lashed his tail, and said to the other cats, "Now what shall we do wid him?" They both answered, "Wait till Emmett comes."

The old preacher looked furtively around, slowly folded up his Bible, put it into his pocket, and said, "Well, gemman, I suttinly is glad to hab met up wid yo' dis ebenin', an' sholy do admire fo' to had yo' company, but when Emmett comes, you tell him I done been heah an' hab done went."

13. STANDING CAT
Artist unknown
mid 19th century
Pennsylvania or Virginia
redware   7"
Collection of Mr. and Mrs. Peter Tillou

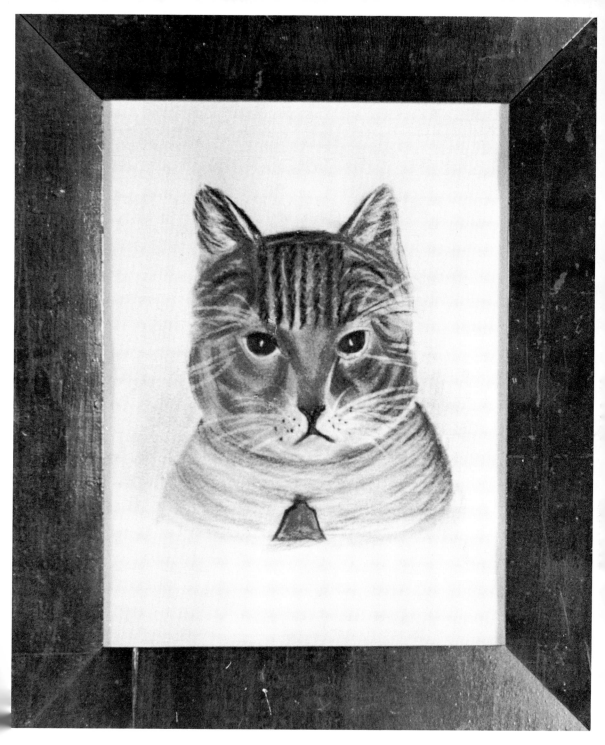

14. TOM CAT
Artist unknown
c. 1850
found in New Jersey
charcoal on paper   6½" x 8½"
Collection of Mr. and Mrs. Burton E. Purmell

15.   MINNIE FROM THE OUTSKIRTS OF THE VILLAGE
      R. P. Thrall
      1876
      found near Woodstock, New York
      oil on canvas   27¼″ x 19¼″
      Courtesy of the Shelburne Museum, Vermont

Grease a cat's feet and it will never run away from home.

16. BLACK AND WHITE CAT
Attributed to Collins Eisenhauer
c. 1955
Nova Scotia
wood, polychromed   13½″
Private Collection

To prevent fits in a cat, let it eat a piece of new dough.

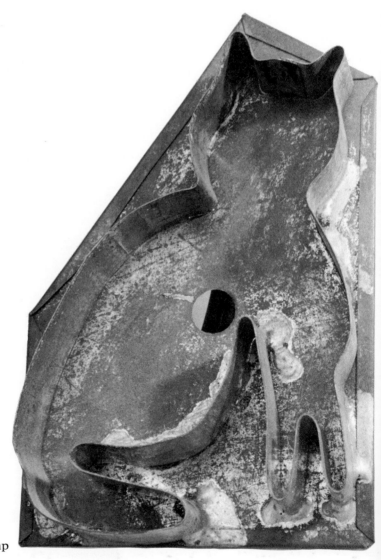

17. COOKIE CUTTER
Artist unknown
1850
Pennsylvania
tin   8″
Collection of Betty M. Trump

18. CAT CONTEMPLATING A FISH BOWL
    Gorman
    1944
    found in New Jersey
    oil on cardboard   12″ x 16″
    Collection of Mr. and Mrs. Joseph Zarro

If a black cat crosses your path, take off your hat and turn it completely around to avoid bad luck.

19. PORTRAIT OF A CAT
Ellen Tall Knouse
1975
New Jersey
reverse appliqué   17½″ x 14½″
Collection of Mr. and Mrs. Wayne Edmund Knouse

20. GIRL WITH CAT *(Miss Catherine Van Slyck Dorr)*
Ammi Philips
c. 1814
oil on canvas   30″ x 25″
Courtesy of the Amon Carter Museum of Western Art,
Fort Worth, Texas

21. BEAN BAG
   Artist unknown
   c. 1890
   embroidered fabric, chain stitched
   3½″ x 3½″
   Collection of Jack and Gretchen Sharp

22. CAT QUILT
Artist unknown
c. 1850
New York
cotton appliqué   88" x 84"
Collection of Lauren Cohen

(Photograph courtesy of America Hurrah Antiques)

23. **PICKING FLOWERS**
Artist unknown
1845
oil on canvas   44½″ x 27½″
Courtesy of the New York State Historical
Association, Cooperstown, New York

24. **GIRL IN RED WITH HER CAT AND DOG**
Ammi Phillips
c. 1834—1836
New York
oil on canvas   32″ x 28″
Private collection

25. MAN, CAT AND MACKEREL
Caleb Purrington
1854
Fairhaven, Massachusetts
oil on canvas   17¼″ x 21½″
Collection of Old Darmouth Historical Society
Whaling Museum; Gift of Mrs. Barbara Johnson

ANN GRAY
Sturtevant J. Hamblen
c. 1843
Massachusetts
oil on academy board   13¾″ x 9¾″
Collection of Mr. and Mrs. Peter Tillou

CAT CHAIR
Artist unknown
20th century
wood, polychromed   19″
Courtesy of Kelter-Malcé Antiques, N.Y.C.

28. CAT WITH MOUSE
     Artist unknown
     mid 19th century
     found in Sunderland, Massachusetts
     watercolor on paper   15½″ x 13″
     Collection of Mr. and Mrs. Kenneth Hammitt

29. SILHOUETTE WITH CAT
Artist unknown
c. 1860
found in New York
hollow cut silhouette and watercolor
5½″ x 4¼″
Collection of Joseph and Janet Wolyniec

RED TIGER CAT WITH THIRTEEN TOES
Artist unknown
c. 1850
New York
oil on board   8½″ x 10″
Courtesy of The Silver Flag

31. GIRL IN RED WITH CAT
Artist unknown
c. 1810
oil   29″ x 24½″
Collection of Mrs. S. Yale Brass

32. ARCHED BLACK CAT
Artist unknown
c. 1930
painted tin   19½″ x 12″
Private Collection

CAT QUILT TOP
Artist unknown
c. 1930
pieced cotton   36″ x 51″
Courtesy of Kelter-Malcé Antiques, N.Y.C.

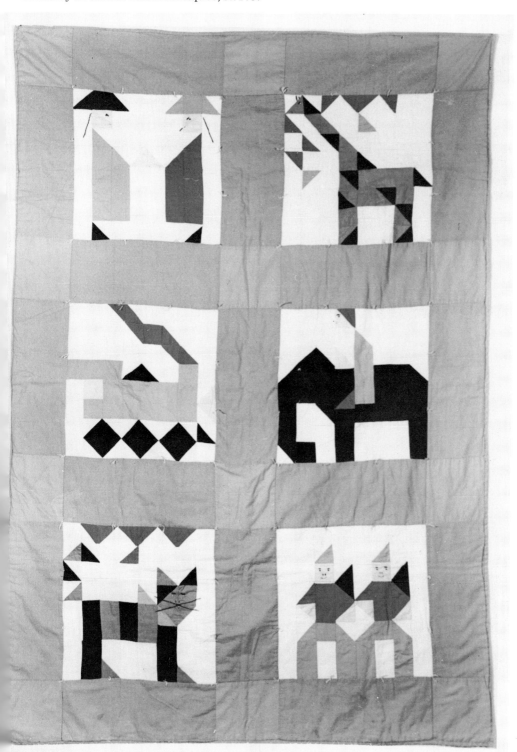

THE HOMELESS ANIMALS

There was a fellow, he was a very poor man once, an' he had an old rooster. So he said to the rooster, "Say, rooster, I'm a pretty ol' man and I kin just make expenses now. You better git yourself a home." So the rooster set out to find a home. On his way he met a dog. He said, "Hello, dog, where you goin'?" The dog said, "Well, my master put me out of his home. I ain't got no more teeth an' I ain't no more good, so he sent me off by myself." The rooster said, "Come on wif me." So the two of them went along an' pretty soon they come across a mule. They said, "Hello, mule, where are you goin'?" He said, "Well, my master sent me off to find a home for myself. I got four big legs all sewed up and couldn't do anything, so my master sent me off." So they said, "Come on, we'll all go together." So they went on an' travelled that night. So they run up on a cat. They said, "Hello, cat, where you goin'?" The cat said, "Well, my master has sent me out to find my own home. I ain't got no more teeth an' I can't catch no rats, so my master sent me away." So they all said, "Come along with us." So they all went along together. They struck a place that night where they gave balls and dances. So the rooster got up in a tree; the mule he got in some hot manure; the dog got under the step; an' the cat got in a corner of the fireplace like he used to do at home; an' they all went to sleep. So pretty soon, someone came to the house an' struck a match. With that, the cat jumped up an' screeched at the man, the rooster set up a loud crowing, the dog grabbed the man by the leg, an' the mule raised up an' kicked the man. So from that time on, no one would go into that house; they claimed that the place was haunted, so that gave them all a home.

Fauset, Arthur Huff. NEGRO FOLK TALES FROM THE SOUTH. Austin, Texas: "The Journal of American Folklore," Vol. 40, July-September, 1927, page 258.

34. LITTLE GIRL IN LAVENDER
     John Bradley
     1840
     oil on canvas   33⅞" x 27⅜"
     National Gallery of Art. Gift of
     Edgar William and Bernice Chrysler Garbisch

You will always be lucky if you know how to make friends with strange cats.

35. CHILD HOLDING A CAT WITH A LEASH
     John Kane
     c. 1929
     oil on canvas   17½″ x 19½″
     Collection of Davida and Alvin Deutsch

6. STUDY IN GRAY AND BLACK
   Artist unknown
   c. 1875
   oil on canvas   30″ x 29″
   Collection of Mr. and Mrs. Dana Tillou

37. MY CHILDREN
Malcah Zeldis
1975
Brooklyn, New York
oil on masonite   20″ x 2
Collection of Malcah Zeldis

38. BLACK CLOTH CAT
Lizzie Brubaker
1973
Pennsylvania
11″ x 8″
Courtesy of America Hurrah Antiques, N.Y

*Made from an old cloth coat
belonging to the artist's sister.*

49.
CRAZY QUILT
Artist unknown
1880
Velvet and fur fabric
67" x 45"
Private Collection

40.

GIRL AND CAT
William Thompson Bartoll
c. 1850
oil on canvas   27" x 22"
Abby Aldrich Rockefeller Folk Art Collectic
Williamsburg, Va.

41.

BOOT SCRAPER
Artist unknown
c. 1890
Found in New York
cast iron   12" x 18"
Collection of Joseph and Janet Wolyniec

THE BLACK CATS' MESSAGE

"The ole man was a wood-cutter. One evenin' as he was comin' home from his work, he saw a passel o' black cats out in the road. He looked to see what they was doin', an' theah was nine black cats totin' a little dead cat on a stretcher. He thought, 'Well, I never heard o' sich a thing as this: nine black cats totin' a little dead cat on a stretcher.'

"Jes' then, one o' them cats called out to the ole man an' says, 'Say, Mistuh, please tell Aunt Kan that Polly Grundy's daid.'

"The ole man nevah answered 'em; he jes' walked on a little peahtah; but he thought, 'Um-m-m! If this ain't the beatin'est thing, them cats a-tellin' me to tell Aunt Kan that Polly Grundy's daid. Who is Aunt Kan, I wonder; an' who is Polly Grundy?'

"Well, he jes' walked on, an' presen'y one of 'em hollered ag'in, an' say, 'Say, ole man, please tell Aunt Kan that Polly Grundy's daid.'

"He jes' walked on ag'in, gittin' a little faster all the time; an' presen'y all of 'em squall out: 'Hey there, ole man, please suh, tell Aunt Kan Polly Grundy's daid.'

"Then the ole man he broke into a run, an' he nevah stopped till he got to his house. He thought he wouldn't tell his ole 'oman nothin' about it. But that night he was settin' befo' de fiah eatin' his suppah—ole folks lots o' times eats dey suppah befo' de fiah—an' while his wife was a-settin' it foh 'im, he say, 'Well, Ole 'oman, I guess I'll tell you some'n dat I didn't think I would tell you.'

"When he say that, the ole yellow cat got up f'om de corner wheres she'us a-layen, an' come ovah an' set down right by his chaiah, a -lookin' up at 'im.

"His ole 'oman say, 'Well, what is it, Ole Man? I knowed they'uz some'n' on you' min' when you come in at dat do'.'

"He say, 'Well, when I 'uz comin' in from de woods dis evenin', walkin' down de road, right theah in de road I seen a whole passel o' black cats. When I went ovah an' looked, theah was nine black cats a-totin' a little daid cat on a stretcher; an' them cats squall out to me three diffunt times an' tell me to tell Aunt Kan that Polly Grundy's daid.'

"When he say that, ole yellow cat jumped up an' say, 'Is she? B'God, I mus' go to the buryin'! 'An' out that do' she flew, an' she ain' nevah come back yit!'"

Dobie, Frank J. SPUR-OF-THE-COCK. Dallas, Texas: Southern Methodist University Press, 1960, pages 99-100.

Julia Ann Merrill. aged 10 Months.
September 4th 1837.

JULIA ANN MERRILL, aged 10 months
Joseph H. Davis
Dated September 4th, 1837
watercolor   5¾″ x 4½″
Collection of Allan L. Daniel

43.   THREE CATS
       Artist unknown
       19th century
       gouache on paper   9¾″ x 13½″
       Collection of the Robert Hull Fleming
       Museum, bequest of Henry Schnackenberg

       This stencil picture was taken
       from a Currier and Ives print

If a cat scratches you, you will be disappointed that day.

44. KITTEN CAUGHT IN KNITTING
Hutchins
1853
Gorham, Maine
watercolor   6½ x 8⅛″
Collection of Joan Samuels

45. FRIGHTENED KITTEN
     Artist unknown
     early 20th century
     found in Concord, New Hampshire
     oil on wooden board   9¾″ x 8¾″
     Collection of Hillary Underwood

46. CAT
     Artist unknown
     20th century
     wood, glass eyes and wire whiskers
     15″ x 18½″
     Collection of Mr. Raymond Saroff

48. MRS. KEYSER
     Artist unknown
     1834
     watercolor   18" x 23"
     Collection of Mr. and Mrs. Burton E. Purm

47. CAT CUT-OUT
     Attributed to George White
     c. 1820
     india ink, watercolor, and pencil
     7⅛" x 9⅛"
     Collection of Mrs. Barbara Chiolino

49. VERMONT CAT
Artist unknown
c. 1870
textile: plush with embroidery
10¼″ x 14″
Collection of George Schoellkopf

A sty may be cured by rubbing it with a black cat's tail.

It is very lucky to have a grey cat pass in front of you.

50. TRAY
     Artist unknown
     19th century
     metal, polychromed   17⅞″ x 24⅛″
     Collection of Mrs. Merril Arden

THE CAT WITH THE WOODEN PAW

Jack Storme was the local cooper and blacksmith of Thebes (Illinois). He had a cat that stayed around his ship. The cat was the best mouser in the whole country, Jack said. He kept the shop free of rats and mice. But one day the cat got a forepaw cut off. After that he began to grow poor and thin and didn't take any interest in anything because he wasn't getting enough to eat.

So one day Jack decided to fix him up a wooden paw. He whittled one out with his knife and strapped it on the maimed leg. After that the cat began to grow sleek and fat again. Jack decided to stay at the shop one night to see how the cat managed it with his wooden paw.

After dark the cat got down in front of a mouse-hole and waited. Pretty soon a mouse peered out cautiously. Quick as a flash the cat seized it with his good paw and knocked it on the head with his wooden one. In no time that cat had eighteen mice piled up before the hole.

Dorson, Richard M. BUYING THE WIND. Chicago, Ill.: The University of Chicago Press, 1972, page 349.

51. SMILING CAT
Artist unknown
early 20th century
wood   4¼″ x 4″
Collection of Howard and Carter Berg

52. THE GIRL WITH TWO CATS
Artist unknown
19th century
oil on canvas   23½″ x 17½″
Collection of Mr. and Mrs. Charles G. Palter

BOY WITH CAT
Attributed to Joseph Goodhue Chandler
c. 1845
oil on canvas   42" x 26"
Collection of Dr. and Mrs. Ralph Katz

54.   GIRL WITH CAT EYEING A BIRD
       Artist unknown
       c. 1800
       watercolor   6⅜" x 7⅛"
       Courtesy of the New York State Historical
       Association, Cooperstown, New York

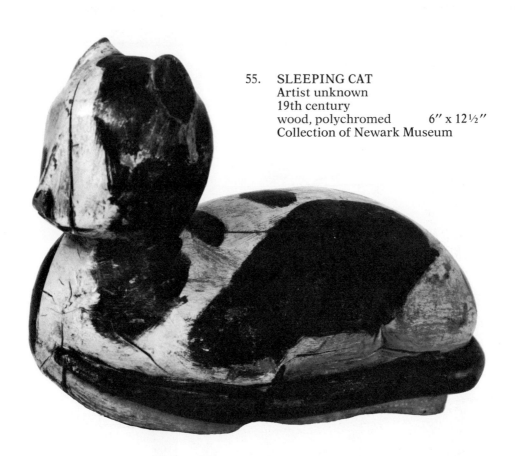

55. SLEEPING CAT
Artist unknown
19th century
wood, polychromed   6″ x 12½″
Collection of Newark Museum

56. MRS. JOSIAH B. KEYLOR'S CAT
Artist unknown
c. 1850
oil on canvas   17″ x 14″
Abby Aldrich Rockefeller Folk Art Collecti
Williamsburg, Va.

"This cat was owned by and, perhaps, pai
by the first wife of Dr. Josiah B. Keylor, (
ran-Bair, nee Keylor, daughter of Dr. Ke
second wife. Picture probably painted by
first wife before marriage or by a local Ch
Co. artist. Arnold R. Beardsley 4/24/69."

57. CHILD AND CAT
     Artist unknown
     c. 1830
     watercolor on paper   12″ x 9½″
     Collection of Davida and Alvin Deutsch

If a cat washes her face in front of several persons, the first person she looks at will be the first to get married.

58. PEDIMENT
Lewis Miller
c. 1830
York, Pennsylvania
wood   11¾″ x 64″
Collection of the Historical Society of York County

The pediment was on Miller's family's home in York, Pennsylvania. When the house was dismantled in 1878 the pediment was removed and later found in York on a back porch.

Cats cannot smell with their whiskers cut off.

59. NUTCRACKER
Artist unknown
early 20th century
wood, polychromed   8¼" x 3¼"
Collection of Joseph S. Caldwell IV

60. GIANT CAT
Artist unknown
20th century
papier mâché   43"
Collection of Mr. and Mrs. Franklyn Litsky

If a neighbor's cat comes listening around your house, it means news-carrying, and you may know that the neighbors are gossiping about you.

61. **STAGES OF MAN'S LIFE**
Artist unknown
signed "MJH"
c. 1850
watercolor, pencil and ink on paper
9 ¼" x 13 ⅜"
Abby Aldrich Rockefeller Folk Art Collection,
Williamsburg, Virginia

*This watercolor is probably copied from
a print by N. Currier of the same title*

62. FENCE POST ORNAMENT
Collins Eisenhauer
c. 1955
Nova Scotia
wood   16″ x 19″
Collection of John Seery

If you see a cat looking out a window, it will storm soon.

63. CAT IN WINDOW
   Artist unknown
   last quarter of 19th century
   oil on canvas   22½″ x 31¼″
   Private collection

64. CROSS-EYED CAT
Artist unknown
20th century
iron   16″
Collection of Burton and Helaine Fendelman

Shape suggests piece was part of an andiron.

65. THE BARBER SHOP
Arthur Cugino
c. 1930
oil on board   10¾″ x 10⅝″
Collection of Barry Cohen

When the pupils of a cat's eyes are nearly closed, it shows that it is low tide, while the widely opened condition signifies high water. In a case in which the pupils of a cat in a Boston barber shop were nearly closed at high water, the barber who owned the cat explained the discrepancy by saying "Oh, well she's only a kitten anyhow and couldn't be expected to know the tide like an old cat."

STALKING CAT
Artist unknown
Early 20th century
wood, polychromed   5¾″ x 24″
Collection of Bernard Barenholtz

67. GRAVESTONE DEPICTING A LONG-HAIRED CAT ON A STOOL
Artist unknown
late 19th century
soapstone, carved in relief   23″ x 13″
found in Bristol, New Hampshire
Collection of the Shelburne Museum, Vermont

It is luck to have a tortoise-shell cat.

68. KITTENS EXAMINING A MOUSE SWIMMING
IN A MILK BOWL
Flora E. Bailey
1883
Turner, Oregon
oil on canvas   12½″ x 16½″
Collection of Mrs. Milton Gardiner

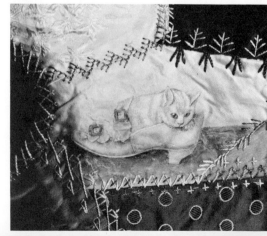

70.   CAT WEATHERVANE
Attributed to C. W. Parker
c. 1930
metal   12″ x 24″
Collection of Mr. and Mrs. Kenneth Milne

Originally made for a carrousel, the cat was later mounted and made into a weathervane.

69.   CRAZY QUILT
Artist unknown
dated 1884
found in Indiana
textile stitched, hand painted and applied
lithographs   57½″ x 58″
Collection of Marcia and Ronald Spark

*To prevent a stray cat from running away, cut some
hair from its tail and wear it in your shoes.*

71. CAT IN THE BOOT
     Artist unknown
     late 19th century
     oil on canvas   11¾″ x 8¼″
     Collection of Mrs. Merril Arden

72.
SIAMESE CAT
Artist unknown
c. 1930—1940
painted wood   11½″ x 3½″
Collection of Susan Gray

73.
CATS PLAYING WITH A SPOOL OF THREAD
Artist unknown
late 19th century
New England
pastel   16″ x 20″
Collection of Dorothy D. McKenney

74. ROCKING CART PANEL
Artist unknown
late 19th century
Connecticut
painted wood   18″ x 25″
Private collection

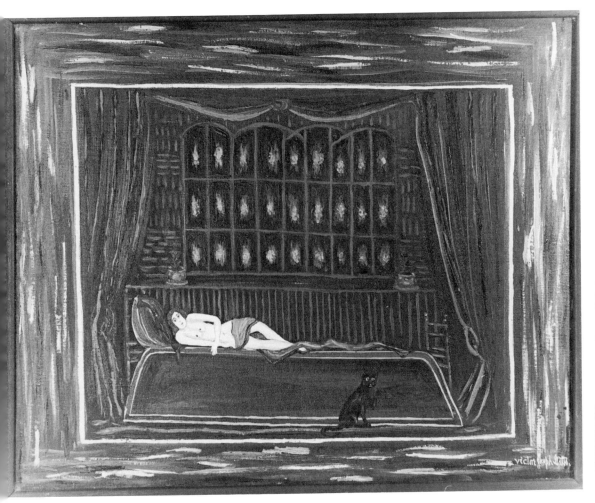

75. CAT HOUSE
Victor Joseph Gatto
c. 1930
oil on canvas   23⅛″ x 29″
Collection of Mr. David L. Davies

PORTRAIT OF A CAT
Artist unknown
c. 1870
found in New York
oil on board   13″ x 9¾″
Collection of Joseph and Janet Wolyniec

77. PAINTED CHEST
Artist unknown
c. 1810—1830
Vermont-New Hampshire origin
painted wood   14″ x 24″
Collection of Mr. and Mrs. Peter Goodman

78. "FULL MOON"
Artist unknown
c. 1930
New York
oil on board   13½" x 18½"
Collection of Herbert W. Hemphill, Jr.

HOW MANY TAILS?

One time there was a fellow by the name of Cal Watson that got to be a great reader, and he talked mighty scientific.

"There's only one way to tell if anything is true," says he, "and that is to reason it out logical."

But Doc Hanberry says that's foolishness, because you can prove any goddam thing by logic, whether it's true or not.

"You take a simple question, like how many tails has a cat got," says Doc. "A cat has got one more tail than no cat at all, ain't it?"

Cal Watson just nodded his head.

"Well," says Doc, "everybody knows that no cat has got two tails."

Cal looked kind of bothered, but finally he wagged his head again.

"All right," says Doc. "Two and one is three, therefore a cat has got three tails!"

Cal Watson opened his mouth twice, but he didn't say nothing.

Doc Hanberry just grinned at him. "That's logic," says he, "and any fool can see where it gets you." And then Doc picked up his little black satchel and walked on down the street.

Cal Watson begun to talk mighty fast then, but the boys all laughed so loud nobody could hear what he was a-saying.

Randolph, Vance. STICKS IN THE KNAPSACK AND OTHER OZARK FOLK TALES. New York: Columbia University Press, 1958, pages 98-99.

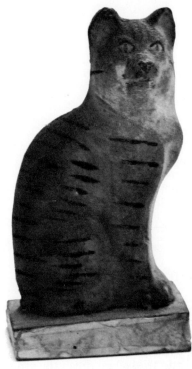

79. SQUEAK TOYS
mid 19th century
papier mâché and felt
6⅞″, 4½″, 6¾″
Collection of Bernard Barenholtz

80. BABY IN BLUE
     Artist unknown
     19th century
     oil on cardboard panel   23⅞″ x 17³⁄₁₆″
     National Gallery of Art. Gift of
     Edgar William and Bernice Chrysler Garbisch

81. ARCHED CAT
Artist unknown
20th century
wood with bristle tail   29″
Private Collection

82. CAKE BOARD
Artist unknown
late 19th century
Pennsylvania
walnut   7¼″ x 11½″
Collection of Betty M. Trump

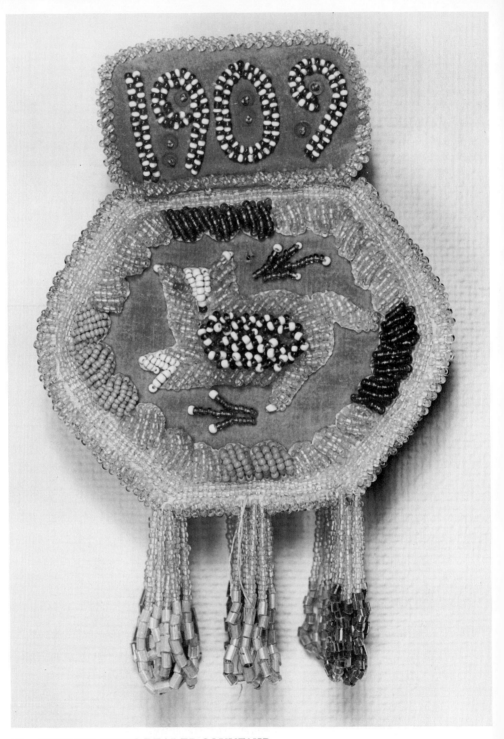

83. NIAGARA FALLS BEADED SOUVENIR
Artist unknown
dated 1909
velvet and glass beads   8½″ x 6¾″
Courtesy of Kelter-Malcé Antiques, N.Y.C.

84. CHOW TIME
Badami
c. 1969
oil on canvas   32″ x 25″
Collection of Mr. Elias Getz

85. CAT IN PARADISE
Jennie Novik
1966
Flushing, New York
oil on canvas   38″ x 41″
Collection of Mrs. Nora Dorn

Origin of the Cat; A Negro Tale.

When I stepped on the cat, her limp and her cries were so piteous, I took her to the kitchen to apologize in a saucer of cream and ask Mammy to care for her.

"Did you trod on dat cat? I certainly is mighty sorry, for it's bound to be unlucky for you if you hurt a cat."

I ventured the opinion that to kill a cat brought ill luck, but had not heard anything about accidentally hurting one.

"My mercy, chile, don't you know it is a sin to kill a cat? Duz you know anything about cats and how they come to be here on this earth?"

I acknowledged my ignorance, unless they were included in the general creation, and procession into the ark.

"Well, white folks don't know nothing 'cept what they reads out a books. Wa'n't no cats in no ark, and it's a sin to kill a cat, 'cause a cat is Jesus' right-hand glove. Jesus was down here once, on this here earth, walking round jest like a man. I 'spects you heerd about that, didn't you? It's all put down in the Bible, they tells me. I never seen it thar, fer I can't read nor write; don't know one letter from the next, but it's all writ down in the Bible, what God sent down from heaven in a bush all on fire right into Moses's hand. Yes, indeed, it is God's own truth, jest as I am telling you. When Jesus was here in this world, He went round constant visiting cullud folks. He always was mighty fond of cullud folks. So one day, He was a walking along and he come to a poor old cullud woman's house. When He went in the door and give her 'howdy,' she stand still and look at him right hard. Then she say, 'Lord' (she never seen nor heerd tell of Him before, but something in her just seemed to call his name), and she kept on looking and looking at Him hard, and she say over again, 'Lord, I is jest mizzable.' Then he say, 'Woman, what you mizzable fer?' Then she say, the third time, 'Lord, I is mizzable, fer the rats and the mice is a eating and destroying everything I got. They's done eat all my corn-meal, and all my meat; they's done eat all my clothes. They's eat holes in my bed, and now they's jest ready to eat me myself, and I am that mizzable, I don't know no more what to do.'

"Jesus he look long time at her, mighty hard, and he say, 'Woman, behold your God!' and then He pulled off his right-hand glove, and flung it down on the floor. Soon as that glove touched that floor, it turned into a cat, right then and right thar, and it began a-catching all them rats, and all them mice, more'n any cat done since when it do its best. Indeed it did, made out of Jesus' right-hand glove, before that woman's eyes—the four fingers for the legs, and the thumb for the tail—and that's the truth 'bout how cats got here. Guess you know now why it's a sin to kill a cat, and 'bliged to be unlucky to hurt one."

6. COUNTRY DANCE
M. E. Ferrill
active 1869—1883
oil on canvas   24⅝″ x 28⅜″
National Gallery of Art. Gift of
Edgar William and Bernice Chrysler Garbisch

When a cat licks its tail, a visitor will come from the direction the tail points.

87. WALL SHELF
Artist unknown
19th century
wood   19″ x 13″
Collection of Bates and Isabel Lowry

88. CAT IN THE WOODS
Artist unknown
found in New Hampshire
late 19th century
reverse painting on glass
12¾" x 15¾"
Collection of Dan Wagoner

89. SCRATCHING POST
Artist unknown
c. 1900
oak with carpeting   38″
Collection of Cecile Singer

90.   BALL-TOSS
Artist unknown
c. 1900
canvas, polychromed   13″
Collection of Burton and Helaine Fendelr

CANE
Artist unknown
c.1890–1910
wood, relief carved cat   37″
Private Collection

BALL-TOSS CAT
Artist unknown
c. 1910
painted canvas   26″
Collection of Barry Cohen

93. BOY IN RED HOLDING WILD-EYED CAT
Artist unknown
c. 1834
oil on canvas   42″ x 24″
Collection of Mr. and Mrs. Peter Tillou

94. BREAKER BOY
Savitsky
1968
oil   8″ x 10″
Collection of Mr. Elias Getz

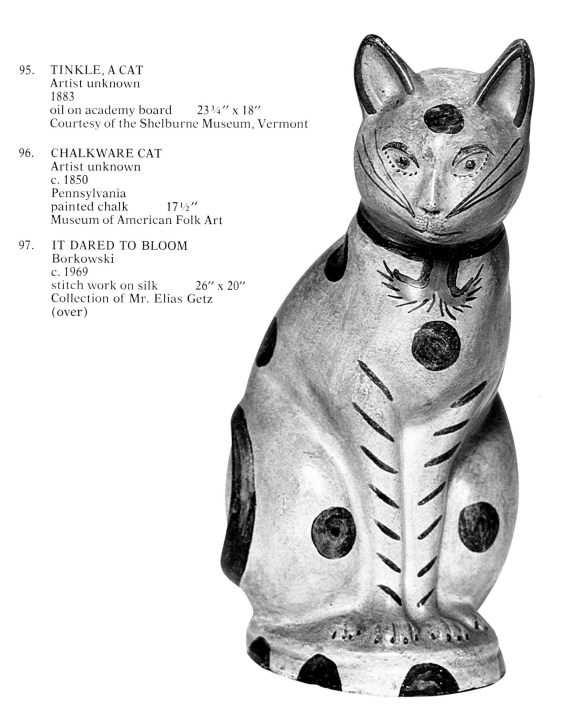

95. TINKLE, A CAT
    Artist unknown
    1883
    oil on academy board   23¾″ x 18″
    Courtesy of the Shelburne Museum, Vermont

96. CHALKWARE CAT
    Artist unknown
    c. 1850
    Pennsylvania
    painted chalk   17½″
    Museum of American Folk Art

97. IT DARED TO BLOOM
    Borkowski
    c. 1969
    stitch work on silk   26″ x 20″
    Collection of Mr. Elias Getz
    (over)

To retain a stray cat, let it see itself in a mirror.

JUST WATCHING
Sali Frantz
1954
opaque watercolor   23½″ x 29″
Collection of Peter B. Frantz

99. PILLOW
     Artist unknown
     early 20th century
     hand painted design on velvet
     12" x 22¾"
     Collection of Hillary Underwood

When walking along the street, if you meet a cat and it follows you, you will secure some money.

If a cat eats grass it is a sign that it is sick.

100.   CAT UNDER OAK TREE
Artist unknown
19th century
hooking and puff work on black linen
26¾″ x 22⅜″
Collection of Brenda and Howard Brody

101. FOUR CATS PLAYING
Artist unknown
mid 19th century
watercolor on paper   10″ x 14″
Abby Aldrich Rockefeller Folk Art Collection,
Williamsburg, Va.

102. SCHOOL FOR KITTENS
Artist unknown
20th century
oil on canvas board   11½″ x 15½″
Private Collection

103. CHILD IN NIGHTSHIRT WITH CAT
Artist unknown
late 1880's
Thornbury, Ontario, Canada
oil on cardboard   9½" x 12¼"
Collection of Mr. and Mrs. Kenneth E. Brooker

104. **CAT JAR**
Paul Cushman
c. 1807—1835
New York
stoneware   9⅝″
Collection of Barry Cohen

105. BLOND INFANT AND GRAY CAT
Artist unknown
c. 1845
oil on canvas   27" x 23"
Private Collection

106. KITTEN PLAYING WITH STRING
Artist unknown
late 19th century
oil on board plate   7¼″ diameter
Collection of Joseph and Janet Wolyniec

107.   CARROUSEL CAT
       Dentzel
       c. 1910
       Germantown, Pennsylvania
       polychromed wood   41½″ x 51″
       Collection of Cecile Singer

108.   ANGORA CAT
       Morris Hirshfield
       dated 1937
       oil on canvas   22⅛″ x 27¼″
       Collection of The Museum of Modern Art

109. CAT ROOT SCULPTURE
Artist unknown
c. 1910
found in Indiana
wood   12″ x 39″
Courtesy of Kronen Gallery, N.

Bring a cat home blindfolded and immediately throw
it into the middle of the bed and it will never leave.

PET CAT.

110. PET CAT
Artist unknown
c. 1880
pencil on paper   10¼″ x 17″
Collection of Mr. and Mrs. Robert Hallock

111. FIREBOARD
Artist unknown
c. 1890
oil on panel   35¼″ x 41½″
Courtesy of the Henry Ford Museum
Dearborn, Michigan

112. TWO CATS AND THREE KITTENS
Artist unknown
c. 1930
hooked rag and burlap   37″ x 69″
Courtesy of America Hurrah Antiques, N.Y.C.

Unwelcome guests will soon arrive if a strange white cat comes to your home.

JERUSHA HOLDING LUCIFER
Artist unknown
c. 1830
Massachusetts
oil on canvas   27″ x 34″
Collection of Mr. and Mrs. Julian L. Gailey

114.   CAT WITH A FLY ON ITS NOSE
James Norman
1960
oil on canvasboard   8″ x 10″
Collection of Agnes Halsey Jones

115. BALL-TOSS CAT
      Artist unknown
      late 19th century
      painted canvas and leather   15″
      Collection of Herbert W. Hemphill, Jr.

116. **PORTRAIT OF A CAT**
Artist unknown
c. 1875—1880
oil on academy board   20″ x 15½″
found in Byron, New York
Collection of Mr. and Mrs. Richard Barons

Inscribed: My cat won first prize at the Genesee County fair.

117.
MOTHER CAT WITH HER KITTEN
Artist unknown
late 19th century
pencil with watercolor wash   8½" x 5
Collection of Jacqueline and Frank Doneg

118. TOY CAT DOLLS
Artist unknown
early 20th century
stuffed fabric   5½" x 5¼"
Private collection

9. DOLL HOLDING A CAT DOLL
Artist unknown
19th century
cloth doll   70″
Collection of Mr. and Mrs. Victor Johnson

120. TABBY CAT LAYING DOWN
Artist unknown
c. 1870
Poughkeepsie, New York
charcoal on paper   36″ x 24″
Courtesy of The Silver Flag

A cat putting a paw over her head means company.

121. CAT IN THE BOX *(Trompe l'oeil)*
     signed Atkins
     dated 1907
     oil on board   12″ x 15½″
     Collection of Cecile Singer

122. MY LITTLE CAT
Artist unknown
19th century
pencil and chalk on paper
11½″ x 9⅝″
Collection of Brenda and Howard Brody

The Museum gratefully acknowledges Darby Bannard, Ellen Blissman, Elaine Eff, Fred Fried, Robert Mills, Cyril Nelson, Jean-Claude Suarès, and Eleanora Walker for the assistance, research and encouragement they put into this book.

Many of the pieces assembled for the exhibition were found with the help of Marna Brill, Burton and Helaine Fendelman, Susan Ferris, Herbert W. Hemphill, Jr., Louis and Agnes Jones, Kate and Joel Kopp, and Scudder Smith for which we are very grateful.

The following individuals, institutions and galleries generously made their pieces available for the exhibition: the Abby Aldrich Rockefeller Folk Art Collection, the Amon Carter Museum of Western Art, Mr. Jack Anspaugh, Mrs. Merril Arden, Mr. Bernard Barenholtz, Mr. and Mrs. Richard Barons, Howard and Carter Berg, Mrs. S. Yale Brass, Brenda Brody, Mr. and Mrs. Kenneth E. Brooker, Joseph S. Caldwell IV, Mrs. Barbara Chiolino, Barry Cohen, Lauren Cohen, Allan L. Daniel, David L. Davies, Davida and Alvin Deutsch, Jacqueline and Frank Donegan, Mrs. Nora Dorn, Burton and Helaine Fendelman, the Robert Hull Fleming Museum, Mr. and Mrs. Julian L. Gailey, Mrs. Milton Gardiner, Mr. Elias Getz, Mr. and Mrs. Peter Goodman, Susan Gray, Mr. and Mrs. Robert Hallock, Mr. and Mrs. Kenneth Hammitt, Herbert W. Hemphill, Jr., Greenfield Village and Henry Ford Museum, Mr. and Mrs. Boyd Headley, Jr., The Historical Society of York County, David and Sue Irons, Mr. and Mrs. Victor Johnson, Agnes Halsey Jones, Dr. and Mrs. Ralph Katz, Kelter-Malcé Antiques, Mr. and Mrs. Wayne Edmund Knouse, America Hurrah Antiques, James Kronen, Mr. and Mrs. Franklyn Litsky, Bates and Isabel Lowry, Dorothy D. McKenney, Steve Miller, Mr. and Mrs. Kenneth Milne, James Mincemoyer, The Museum of Modern Art, National Gallery of Art, Newark Museum, New York State Historical Association, Old Dartmouth Historical Society Whaling Museum, Mrs. Charles G. Palter, Mr. and Mrs. Burton E. Purmell, Joan Samuels, Mr. Raymond Saroff, George Schoellkopf, John Seery, Jack and Gretchen Sharp, Shelburne Museum, Dr. and Mrs. Alexander Shevlin, Ships of the Sea Museum, The Silver Flag, Cecile Singer, Marcia and Ronald Spark, Mr. and Mrs. Dana Tillou, Peter Tillou, Betty M. Trump, Hillary Underwood, Dan Wagoner, Dr. H. J. Waldman, Joe and Ellen Wetherell, Joseph and Janet Wolyniec, Mr. and Mrs. Joseph Zarro, and Malcah Zeldis. We thank them and the anonymous lenders.

123.   GIRL IN BLUE WITH WHITE CAT
Artist unknown
c. 1820
found in New York
oil on canvas   16″ x 20″
Collection of Mr. and Mrs. Burton E. Purmell

The folk stories included in this book come from the following sources:

Coffin, Tristram P. and Cohen, Hennig. FOLKLORE IN AMER-
ICA. Garden City, New York: Doubleday and Company,
1966, pages 26-28.

Dobie, Frank J. SPUR-OF-THE-COCK. Dallas, Texas: Southern
Methodist University Press, 1960, pages 99-100.

Dorson, Richard M. BUYING THE WIND. Chicago, Ill.: The
University of Chicago Press, 1972, page 349.

Fauset, Arthur Huff. NEGRO FOLK TALES FROM THE
SOUTH. Austin, Texas: "The Journal of American Folklore," Vol. 40, July-September, 1927, page 258.

Randolph, Vance. STICKS IN THE KNAPSACK AND OTHER
OZARK FOLK TALES. New York: Columbia University
Press, 1958, pages 98-99.

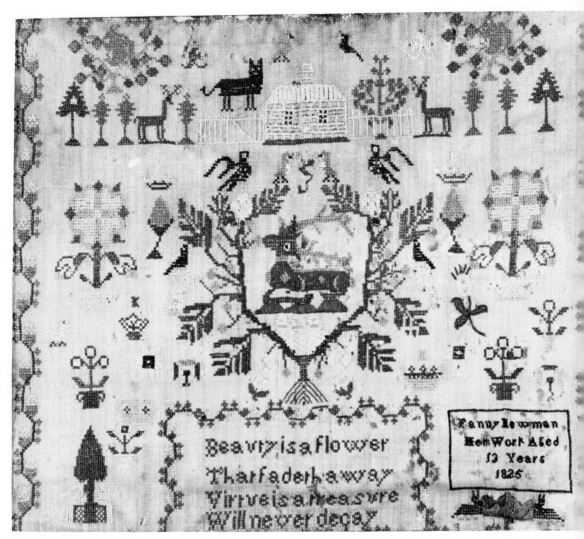

Beauty is a flower
That fadeth away
Virtue is a treasure
Will never decay.

Fanny Newman
Her Work Aged
13 Years
1825

124. SAMPLER
Fanny Newman
1825
linen   10⅜″ x 12⅝″
Collection of David and Sue Irons

9-2977

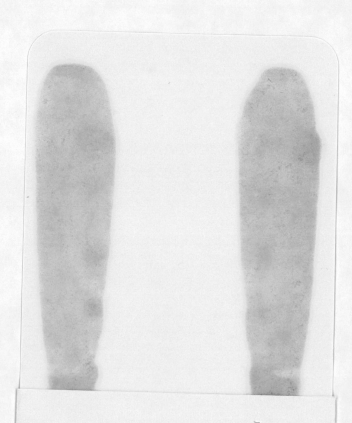